Far Flung

Dean Thomas Ellis

Portals Press

Tower of Babel cover art is a photographic reproduction (via fineartamerica) of an anonymous painter from the 16th/17th C Flemish school

Interior illustrations © 2022 by Selina McKane

Grateful acknowledgments: Some of the poems in this collection have appeared in the following publications: *The Iron Lattice, The Maple Leaf Rag, Truck* and *St. Petersburg Review*. Special thanks to Jodi Campbell for her invaluable eye in the preparation of this volume, Selina McKane for her skilled hand and artistry, JP Travis for his spirit and encouragement, and Amarilis for her constant and ingenuous inspiration. And for Mom. — DTE

Far Flung by Dean Thomas Ellis
ISBN 978-0-9970666-6-1
Published by Portals Press
New Orleans, Louisiana, USA
www.portalspress.com

Table of Contents

Far Flung

Babel

"Por una vez sobre la tierra
no hablemos en ningún idioma,
por un segundo detengámonos,
no movamos tanto los brazos."

For once on the face of the earth,
let's not speak in any language;
let's stop for one second,
and not move our arms so much.

— Pablo Neruda, "A callarse"

A collapsed tower gobbled
by the tides all the world's
weight in the belly of a ghost
ship the hull scraped of syntax
dialects dangling from dead
branches calcify on salt
sweet tongues that speak
only to themselves the sole
response a cratered resolution
written in a thousand lost
languages by the legislature
of the sea with no hope
of passing crashes to
the shore swallowed
by sandworms

Slippers

Strange silence, signifier
of the sacred. Footsteps
approach. Indistinct chatter.
Sound is at once accidental
and intentional, a recitation
without rhyme.

To be physically undone,
bewept, by the threadbare,
the miraculous, the terrible
gravity of words, by traces
left in the margins of letters
read aloud to absent lovers.

Poems are but knots of yarn
that seek unraveling. One
can find the whole truth
of the world in one's
slippers.

Forecast

Old woman
in red striped
shirt plays blues
piano in the coffee
house.

Vase of yellow
flowers sits on
the mantle.

Her dirty blonde
hair is tied up
in a bun. Dusk
has fallen. No
one listens,
everyone
scribbles.

Tonight there
will be a meteor
shower.

Alley

"Oblivion as they rose shrank like a thing reproved."
— Percy Bysshe Shelley

There was an alley
an owl a bitter moon.

There was also
a cat and a man
with a cane.

Come to think
of it perhaps
I read it in
a book by a
Persian poet
perhaps whose
name perhaps
was Moshiri
and perhaps
yes I dreamt
the rest.

And perhaps
the poem and
the dream had
something to do
with an alley
the same one
we walked
before you
saw me off.

Yet I don't
recall us
having met.

Metro Page: Menagerie

Mischievous marsupial
stands accused of many
sins, ducks the allegations,
snorts a reluctant apology
through flared nostrils.

Hirsute herbivore
buckles under
the weight of
the charges.

Lanky lion roars
its defiant roar,
says yeah, so
I'm guilty, so
what?

*Whattaya gonna
do about it?*

Proper
pachyderm
crushes
the lion
underfoot.

Plum/Holocaust (after Abraham Sutzkever)

What can you wrest
from a plum? Nest
eggs, barbed wire,
shaving cream, gum
wrappers. Challah
knots, a snatched
purse, parchment.
Loaves purple as
bullets, mezuzahs
stuffed with spiders.
The chirp of craven
men mourning their
mothers, the brio
of their breathing.
Catcalls of soldiers,
kerosene-blood
spilling from
lamps the cry
of cymbals
echoing off
the windowpanes.

Then there's
the pit: sluiced,
hard, unyielding,
yielding. Smash
it with poetry
and out will ooze
the mauve reproach
of memory, ether
of candlewax,
elixir of lost
language:

One bird escapes the nest
  one nest escapes the tree
    one tree escapes the forest
      one forest escapes the Earth

  the Earth is bereft of birds

Lemon (after Yi Sang)

the poet asks for a taste
of lemon on his deathbed
a smidgeon of sour to
ease the sweet release
into eternity but lemon
is no longer available
in wartime Tokyo all
trees bartered to the
enemy in exchange
for the promise to
spare the hospital
in which he dies
but the scrawny
nurse with the
skeletal legs
and aqueous
eyes kisses
him on the
forehead
the taste of
her trickled
tears soothes
his soon silent
tongue and
that is
enough.

a tree sprouts at his grave.
it yields lemons.

Dream Girl (Hothouse)

She treads — butterfly boots,
gnarled knees — in the garden,
crushes everything, spares
nothing (except the butterflies).

I sip ether — sweet, turned,
lemon brown — on the porch,
heedless of the carnage.

Her stealthy entrance, clumsy
against the millwork, upends
the perfect lines, the tilled
promise I've sown
into the earth.

I retreat to the shotgun,
drink her hothouse poison,
sleep in my hothouse dreams.

In the morning I find
the newspaper lying
in a boneyard.

Butterflies flutter at its edges,
announcing its banal
catastrophes.

Flannery

A crutch, a cross,
the criminal heart in
the sweltering South.
A precise mind conjures
a messy redemption; she
limps to the porch for afternoon
tea. A flat forelock falls against
her cheek; she spits out a peacock
feather. She climbs on a tractor, wipes
her face with a red bandana, tastes
sweat in the crook of her good arm.
Swollen ankles bulge from high
green heels; she takes no solace
in the twisted allure. She writes
more than she reads; regards
the man at the altar. Shame
on you, Jesus, she says.

The only atonement
I seek is my own.

UPON FALLING ASLEEP WHILE READING
THE QUIET AMERICAN OR MAYBE WHILE
WATCHING THE FILM VERSION NOT THE ORIGINAL
BUT THE SUPERIOR REMAKE WITH MICHAEL CAINE
OR MAYBE IT WAS *THE LOVER* BY MARGAURITE DURAS
OR MAYBE IT WAS THE FILM VERSION

Once I rode a rickshaw
with Graham Greene he
told me, as the driver's
vertebrae creaked forward,
and groaned a doleful
chorus with the wooden
wheels, you suffer as much
as the driver, you see, because
you are his burden and he
yours. It took me years
to learn this, he said, and
I am still learning. But why
then, I asked, do you still
take rickshaws? Because,
he said, they need my business
and I am too lazy to walk. And
then I awoke from the bubble-
wrapped dream, and tore
the cellophane from my eyelids,
and knew, quite unknowingly,
that I would never ride
a rickshaw, or know anyone
who ever knew anyone who
knew Graham Greene.

Poem (for Forugh Farrokhzad)

"One window is enough for me."

Buried beneath the February
snows she is the verse she
never wrote the one willed
to her faithless lovers
in the hard loam
of each caress
the sweet scrape
of each kiss
the dissident dance
of each resistance

against absent
rib broken by
the pushing
against itself
every crack
an amulet
slicing the rigid
skin of silence
the quest for exile
in the homeland
an exile never
reached except
by burial beneath
the February snows.

One Papish Cat: A Prayer for L.F.

"with his head cocked sideways
                    at streetcorners"
                 — Lawrence Ferlinghetti

The poem alone on a bare
                    stage. Blackbirds circle
overhead a cawing choreography of
                    darkness and drift
circadian and ceaseless
                    defrocked and ordained
    what ain't and what is
                    the poem gazing skyward
        iambic uprooted foresakes
                    its own
                    lines tosses the script
into the proscenium
                    improvs a monologue
a rat-a-tat riff
                    a where y'at scat
a whataboutthat
                    a complex chord reduced
to piquant paste sweet to the
                    eartaste then   ambles
its skeletal frame into the
                    birdless wings
as the audience of one papish cat
                    yowls its approval
            and rewards the performance
    with silent sustained
                    applause
the poempoet the
                    poetpoem alone
on a bare
        stage

The Safe (Cornish, NH)

"Poets are always taking the weather so personally."
— J.D. Salinger

An unwritten sentence,
perfect arc, drawn across
the handle by the welder's
soft torch. It cuts around
the knob, throws sparks
onto fields of dead brown
rye. Blast of oxygen,
stink of recluse rot,
calcified adolescence.
The slag remains;
hard, implacable.

Once again
the flame, once
again the refusal.
The fields catch fire,
sizzle, unleash bursts of
mortar fire and taxi horns.
Experts gather, pluck up
the strewn pages, shake
their heads, seeing only
the squalor. They leave
the room, dial up
their publishers
with the news
of the final
silence.

The welder removes
the mask, places a red
hunter's hat over his
prematurely grey hair.

Immigrant

Steeped in cold
county

Sweet burlesque of
privation

She speaks, to
America

Lilt of syllable
dropped

From her green
tongue

Strafes the
harbor

With jagged
truths

Finds a one room
flat

On the outskirts of
town

Lives, huddled
mass

Yearning to
breathe

Ventriloquism

"Why did the deceased stop visiting this room?"
— Polina Barskova

The Russian poets
declaim their poems
in unclipped syllables
on the video screen
of the old Armory
that once served
during the Siege
as detention center
and torture chamber
but that was eons ago
and those things
don't happen
anymore

well anyway not so
much not so anyone
would notice except
perhaps the litter
of cats that mew
echoes of the screams
their ancestors mewed
decades ago when all
words were not as
unpronounceable
as they are today

Okinawa, September, 1945

The comfort woman
gave him no little
discomfort stupid
    soldier snatched
from suburban
    America
and sent to kill
    any number
of her brethren
    and having done
    his duty
steeps now in the sweet
    bound shadow
of her reproof

Diaspora, or: God is My Co-Conspirator

"for a Jew he saw in you, not a Buddhist"
— Rodger Kamenetz

Here I sit, in the poetry
section clutching
a curious volume
about the Jews.

A professor-poet takes T.S.
to task: he has lowered all
their cases, called them *jews,*
not Jews. Then he gores
Ginsberg for pardoning
Pound: "How could the
greatest Jew in po'bizness,"
asks the latest Jew in
 po'bizness, "forgive
 the Fascist?" *Oy*
vey ismier.

I was a Jew once. Or so
I'd been told. My father
fiddled with the mezuzah
in the doorway, and said:
"To be Jewish, son, is like
playing centerfield for the
Yankees. More is naturally
expected of you."

But my father expected
nothing of himself: he
didn't know the Talmud
from the Torah the Sukkot
from the Sabbath a *mitzvah*
from a *shiksa.* He married
the latter and, in subsequent
years, recited the Hanukkah

prayer, head covered by
a handkerchief, with his
eldest son, a *leprecohen,*
in a rote of butchered
Hebrew:
Ba-RUCK a-TAW
ah-de-NOY
el-oo-HAY-noo.
may-LECK
ha-o-LAM.

Then we drove off to watch
Fiddler on the Roof
in a suburban cinema,
munching Raisinets,
while survivor
women sniffled
into their hankies.

In South America
the Jewish boys, at *bar*
mitzvah time, are taken
to whorehouses by their
single uncles. Sexual
synagogues; the brothels
have more than a secular
purpose. The *putas,*
afterwards, invoke
the rabbi's words:
"Now, my son, you
are a man."

At 13, I had no *bar*
mitzvah, no confirmation.
My mother refused it;
my father was away,
on business, in South
America. I kissed a girl
named Carol behind

the synagogue, my fingers
grazing the *tzitzis* that draped
her Jewish bosom. She wore
a short skirt and smelled
of codfish and plum wine.
She was my *sukkot,* my
seder, my Sabbath,
the sheath into God's
great world.

Months later, opiated
by Bubbe's brisket,
we lay prone in my
uncle's bedroom,
calculating the sins
we'd amass until
the Day of Atonement,
weeks away. My
father whooped from
the La-Z-Boy in the den.
I wondered if the Giants
had just scored a touchdown.
Israel was dropping bombs
on Lebanon.

One January morning
we tossed dirt together
on my grandfather's
casket. It landed with
a heedless thump,
the ground frozen,
obdurate. The grave
refused the shovels,
the rabbi's prayer
muzzled by
the jackhammer.

"He never made
things easy," said

my father. Then we
drove off to a nearby
diner, and ordered
milkshakes and club
sandwiches, hold
the fries.

My father, who as a child
fasted on Yom Kippur
and spent the day praying
in *shul,* walking the two
miles to the synagogue,
now popped in to say
a prayer for his dead
parents, and drove
back home to treat
himself to a bacon
cheeseburger. "What
difference does it
make now?" he'd say,
mulling over the sports
page, cursing the Giants.
"This bread your mother
buys at the Shop Rite. So
farshtunkene," conjuring
the Yinglish that Abraham,
his father, sweat-stained
from his day at the dry
cleaning shop, intoned to
Elsie, sweat-stained from
her day in the kitchen.

Elsie was from Minsk,
Abraham from a vanished
town in Belarus. My father
invoked The Vanishing
as often as he could,
wearing the number six
million on his chest,

one million fashioned
on each point of the
Star. The Vanishing,
attended by no one he
knew, he pronounced:
Holly-cost, his chest
swelling with pride, and
my mother corrected him
each time: "It's *Holocaust,*
Jerry, and twenty million
Russians died." I'll take
your six and raise you
twenty. She was not
even Russian. He
tried to sneak us
out of the house to
take us to Hebrew
school, to prepare
us for the *aliyah*
never to come,
but she stopped
us at the back
door.

Would the poet-professor,
take my father to task
for turning me, his eldest
son, into a "lowercase jew"?
Or would he call me
a product of my
environment?

Once I saw Elie
Wiesel, the greatest
Jew in Shoah-business,
give a reading at the
University. He spoke,
brow unfurrowed, of
unspeakable things.

The moderator, flush
with implication, asked for
questions. I, quaking with
shame, raised my hand:

"How can one be a Jew
in the American suburbs?
How does one attain
the Bliss of Persecution?
Where is the connective
to Cataclysm tucked
between Banana
Republic and Johnny
Rockets?"

The Greatest Witness
wrinkled his brow,
nodded, and said:

"To be a Jew is not to suffer.
It is to *respond* to suffering.

Continue to respond and you
continue to be a Jew."

And so I sit in the poetry
section, clutching a curious
volume about the Jews. I
am in a bookstore Uptown.
The salesgirl is a serious-looking
shiksa. She asks me if she can
help. "I don't know," I say.
She smirks and returns to
her database and her text
messages, leaving me to
the Diaspora, the sacred texts,
the cryptic lines about faith
and displacement.

Diaspora II: Knish (Inbetweenities)

I once read the Kethubim, she told me, as
she gazed longingly at the potato knish
I had prepared her, with, being only half
Jewish, all the kosher love I could muster.
I imagined my Bubbe Elsie, in her sensible
shoes, nodding with approval at my attempt
to impress this *shiksa* from Nebraska, in her
senseless shoes, now gobbling up the knish
with all the loving intent she once scoured
those extant texts concerning the bewitched
and weak-chinned king of Spain. She taught
European history, somewhere deep in
the unvaccinated heart of Texas, immunized
as it was from reason, and told me, as she
licked her lips with saucy Calvinist
delight, that she knew more about
the kosher slaughtering of animals than
the average bear. What do bears,
I wondered, know about slaughter,
outside of their own, gentile, variety,
and imagined my Bubbe shaking
her soup-scented wig with deferential
consternation, knocking it into the ancestral
broth with handwrung tremors of
inbetweenity, the same lineal shivers
I had inherited from the *goyishe* womb
of my own dear mother. Yet I had
long embraced the inbetweenity
with impunity, and given
the opportunity, took comfort
in the immunity generously
granted by such delights that the cute
shiksa prof, steeped in Spanish history
and kosher butchery and passingly
intimate knowledge of the Kethubim,
presently offered me. She was smiling,
now, with post-knish quietude, a look

28

I hoped to see somewhat later, after
our walk on the levee, which, as I
anticipated, she ardently and lovingly
suggested. And there on the levee,
it began, and later, on the levee,
it ended, with a lot of knishes
inbetween.

Babel II

"When you rip the cloth off the umbrella,
is the umbrella still an umbrella?"
            — Paul Auster

She teaches a class in ancient
abstraction the luminous leak
of secrets between slackened
tongues her students babble
beneath a tower of shadows
splintered by the indistinct
murmur of the waning
moon.

Random pages tossed from a high
tower. One lands as a broadside,
another a screed, a third a bulletin,
another a testament. A proposal,
a proclamation, a potboiler,
a prayer.

An affidavit, an anecdote.
A manifesto, a manuscript.

Children render origami
boats from the refuse,
prophets fashion whole
religions from the pulp,
scholars make hay with
the scraps. Lovers pass
ephemeral valentines,
the rest are swept
into the sewers.

Some swirl in the November
wind, never landing, until
all language is irrelevant.

The Date (Critics)

I wanted to adore
it, she said, as we
left the cinema
that first night.
The film left
traces on her
grey pupils.

I filled in
the rest until
they burned blue.
The next movie
was better. Her
eyes, bedewed,
filled with green
tears.

A Good Rutabaga Is Hard To Find

On the day we are wed
the news is told
that the end
is nigh

And still we cannot
find the proper
way to mark
the occasion

We bike the levee
to buy a rutabaga
at the final farmer's
market

Swede neep snagger
the farmer tells my
wife it has many
names

My wife tells the farmer
her mother made soup
from the peelings
in the camps

But the prisoners
often rejected it
dined on hunger
instead

The farmer nods
and says rutabagas
have a complex
taxonic history

We ask him what
that means he says

he doesn't know he
read it on Wikipedia

We buy three of them
one for her one for me
one for the rest of
Humanity

We don't know how
to prepare them so
we Google *rutabaga*
on the first day of our

marriage and the last
day of Google it says
Finns cook the tuber
in a variety of ways:

roasted baked boiled
uncooked and thinly
julienned it is also
the major ingredient

in the popular
Christmas dish
lanttulaatikko

We laugh about
the word "Finn"
on this day of
all days take
turns saying
lanttulaatikko

Rutabagas says
Google are often
served with
clapshot cawl
tatties and haggis

We sing *clapshot*
cawl tatties and
haggis clapshot
cawl tatties and
haggis clapshot
cawl tatties and
haggis clapshot
cawl tatties and
haggis

My wife claims her mother
who was Hungarian never
cooked rutabagas at home
I ask if it was because of

the camps
no she says
it was because
of the rutabagas

I cut into the purple skin
slice the yellow flesh
into two thin discs

We bite into the raw
hard root and await
the fire

Skeeball (Seaside Heights Boardwalk, 1974)

I held it, firm grip
giving way, yielded
to roundness, wooden
allure, spherical power
remaking my fingers
into an arc

She stood behind
me, mottled by
sand-sleep and
cheap wine, her
fingers slack,
then hard on my
shoulder,
the Everything
I'd dreamed now
an Actual Thing
as real as the
wooden orb in my
palm the salt in my
skin the traffic on
the Parkway the
surf the skywriter
the sweetburn on
my neck her
quivered
breath

later on the beach
the undulations
the cresting
collapsing
swelling sea
all before
she did or
would
or might
but still

she held tight to
my shoulder her
lovely burgeoning
breath a life nascent
on my neck and
the world said

let go let go let
go and my fingers
flew from my
body and my
body gave and
my fingers gave
and the wooden
ball the dark
brown globe
that held
the Earth hit
the alley and

rolled
rolled
rolled and
plunked
its way
to bed.

A bell
rang a ticket
trickled out I
traded it for
a stuffed giraffe
and drove
the three
of us
home.

Labyrinth

"though the shy tilt of the head is uncanny"
— Anthony Lane, review of "Spencer"

There is no wind when I propose
marriage to the shorthaired woman
in the cat-eye glasses. She tilts
her head, just so, when I ask,
while we sit on our usual bench
beside the Labyrinth, that tiled
utopian circle, indicating, with
that tilt, an alluring ambivalence
that says, in effect, yes and no
at once. This, of course, only
enchants me further, imbuing
my proposal with more urgency,
more oomph. I suddenly feel like
I really mean it.

She looks me dead in the eye,
smiles, and the topic never
comes up again.

The wind kicks up, shaking
clumps of Spanish moss off
the oaks. One lands on her lap.
She picks it up and sets it atop
her head, rendering her the
longhair she has always
aspired to be.

We giggle adolescent
giggles, and I kiss my
new, mosshaired
fiancée.

Over by the Tree of Life, the great
spreading oak behind the zoo,
a wedding party cheers. We
don't know them, but the
bride and groom look,
from this distance across
the cosmos, an awful
lot like us.

Second Avenue

She draped herself
on the 3rd floor
landing like poison
ivy: alluring, toxic,
contagious. I climbed
the spiral to a level
where that allure made
sense, where I could
judge it from a safe
distance, yet still
draw in the essence,
get high on the fumes.
I failed, slipped on
the banister and fell
at her feet, curled into
them like an alleycat
into a wound, lapping
at its sweet reproach,
ingesting the catnip
of her lessons. They
tasted like rain. I stood,
and faced my foe; she
smiled the smile of a
television actress, and
spat out her delicious
contagion:

"Hello neighbor. Will
you help me with
my groceries?"

I (good neighbor) nodded
and complied. She led
me inside. Mail piles
up now, on my doorstep,
and the Chinese delivery
boy wonders where I am.

Helena de Brasilia

the woman who lives in a crevice
    that appears to the naked eye as a garden
somewhere on the outskirts of the capital
    designed by the genius architect
a soup bowl a parallelogram a broken abstraction
    modeled after Paris that looks nothing
like Paris but she appears in her crevice a warmaking Helen
    and I appear as Menelaus though I am no king
when she greets me in her garden with her long brown fingers
    wielding cold green legumes plucked
out of the body of the russet earth with the hands
    she refuses me to the point of abstraction
from that crevice in which she lives
    that appears to me as a naked garden
somewhere on the outskirts of the physical world
    far beyond which there are crevices
but this is not the real world this is the false capital
    of the false city built beside a false lake the savannaed
utopia become dystopia but she has found her crevice that
    appears to the naked eye as a garden

Bordel, Belém do Pará, Brasil

Antonia com a boca torcida
Tem nada mais que Celia das estrias
Tem nada mais que Fatima dos olhos vesgos
Cheios de aço e da alvorada cinzenta
Tem nada mais que Joanna das Ruas
Rasgando amantes atrás da catedral
Tem nada mais que Isabella e sua gemea Siames
Separadas desde nascimento. Conheço as duas:
Uma sae de noite, a outra de dia
As duas se chamam Isabella e nenhuma tem mais
(Ate que fazem muito bem os papeis)
Que Antonia com a borca torcida.

Brothel, Belém do Pará, Brazil

Antonia with the twisted mouth
has nothing on Celia with the stretch marks
has nothing on Fatima with the cockeyes
steely and full of the leaded dawn
has nothing on Joanna of the Streets
rending concealed lovers behind the cathedral
has nothing on Isabella and her Siamese twin
unattached since birth. I know them both:
one comes out at night, the other in the day
both named Isabella and neither has anything
(though they act their parts very well)
on Antonia with the twisted mouth.

The Lover (Island)

She is yellow, burnt, mustard, scorched sunset, tiger tail, morning pancake, island mud, Crayola crayon, sweet disease of the skin. I drink down the juice of her, fresh-squeezed, soursop, teeth-tingling. Our colors knit together, a quilt of unraveled secrets, blanketing all wounds, patchwork promises. We meet in the City, hike bald mountains, swim in the drained rivers of her lost nation. Verses appear and vanish, reappear. Her life is a legend, mine a voyage on a listing ship, that she rights with one long, sloping look. We marry in the garden of the family museum, her grandmother's ghost our stern-eyed minister. We live in two languages, die in a thousand, speak in only one.

Her Beauty is

to look over a cliff
and gaze at the river
glistening below
wanting to
jump

and then to
forget the
precipice.

Levitation (Island)

She teeters, daughter
of dusk, cousin to
the mango, on legs
tendered by *merengue*

elbows poised, her
whole island self
gives to the swivel,
miracle maneuver

that brings everything
upward, and forward—
pupil become teacher,
exile become home—

a stretch that finds
womanhood burgeoning
in the branches, the pale
dawn glimmering on

upcast cheeks; no tempest
in sight the riddle
of arrival etched into
mestizo eyes. The fruit

holds in the branches,
the flowers want plucking,
she reaches—ankles, knees,
torso, elbows—and teases

out a mainland life. She
lifts herself, comes into
view of beachcombing
boys and country crooners

who sing bygone boleros.
She grasps for a flower
and breaks a thousand
hearts.

Fix/Model

bleak street

       four miles

outa town

       is where

she finds

       her juju

in cold form

       of needle

and juice

       she shoots

tercets into

       the blank slate

of her veins

       carves quatrains

onto her wrists

       declaims verses

in oozing syllables

       against the hollow chasm

of sleep

Requiem: Tierra del Fuego

What shall I do
with you when
you die? Shall
I cremate you
and carry you
around in a vial
around my neck
or in my vagina?
You should make
your wishes known.

Shall I slice my
cheeks with
your razor cut
your image
into mine
tattoo a selfie
onto your tomb?
You should make
your wishes known.

Shall I mourn
you with tears
or sighs
considering
the fact that I
used to sob
after we
screwed?
You should make
your wishes known.

Shall I call your
boss your barber
your doctor your
dentist? Shall I
tell your students

you're inside
my insides,
on sabbatical?

Shall I dance
with your ghost
on the porch at
noon?
The neighbors
will think I've
gone mad.
Perhaps I have.

Shall I craft a clever
eulogy and not speak
it? Shall I serve
your friends bologna
sandwiches on rye
with Gulden's
mustard, since,
though you would
never admit it,
that was your
favorite?
You should make
your wishes known.

Shall I sleep
with your
brother
or your
wife? Who
will share
the most
secrets?
Shall I take you
to the taxidermist
and have
you stuffed?

I can keep you
in the kitchen,
slather secret
sauce on your
stupid lips.

Shall I bury you
with your pen,
the one I'm using
to write this
poem?
You should make
your wishes known.

I've awakened to
you not awake.
This is something
that would have
amused you.

Shall I bury you
in a coffin covered
with the flag
of Argentina,
since you'll be
heading south
for the winter
spring summer
fall? You've
made it to
Tierra del
Fuego at last
you bastard.

Shall I sit
shiva until
your best friend
comes over,
drunk, and tries
to fuck me,

like always,
and reveal
to him that your
Jewishness was a
ruse to seduce me?
Shall I sing that
song you always
sang in the car,
the one you
knew I hated,
but sang anyway?
Shall I set it to
Amazing Grace
or Pop Goes
The Weasel?
You should make
your wishes known.

Dried tears
are etched
into my
cheeks. A
train could
ride on those
tracks. And
probably
will.

Shall I lie with
other men?
Which ones?
Are there
others?
And all those
books you never
read on the shelves
you never dusted?
Who will they
now impress?

Shall I act stoic
or vengeful? Be
Jackie O or Jackie
Chan? Shall I
recede into sweet
grief or spring
into sham
hysterics?

And what of your
clothing? Shall
I wear it over
mine? Shall I
wear it under
mine? Shall
I wear it instead
of mine? Shall
I burn it and
light your leftover
Camels off the pyre?
You should make
your wishes known.

There is
a cold
bruise on
my shoulder.
Did your
ghost bite
me in my
sleep?
Tell him he
missed his aim.

Shall I drink
coffee at night
and wine in
the morning?
Everything

is upside
down.

Shall I spread
your ashes
on a Ouija
board and see
if they come
up with Yes?
You should make
your wishes known.

In our bed
there are
stains. I
can no
longer tell
the difference
between your
blood and mine.

Babel III

  ghosts in the parlor
whisper sweet
somethings into
  unsealed ears
layer flayed secrets
onto realms of
  cratered streets
pockmarked passions
  green dreams loose
the guileless
logic of grown
  children clinging
to yet unbroken
    promises

Desiccant

The desert knows
what the sea does not:

It knows where the water
is, because there is little water.

It knows where the stars
are, because they bring light
when there is no light.

It knows where the wildlife
hides, where there is no sanctuary.

The sea, with all its abundance,
sleeps under the stars, lets the fish
scamper through, paying them no mind,
knows not the temperance of drought.

The sea, for all its creatures, knows
not how to seek them out.

The sea is a spendthrift,
the desert a miser.

I am the sea, she
is the desert.

And sometimes
the other way
around.

Evacuation Day

When the news came
we fled in all directions:
north to the lake
south to the Gulf
west to the swamp
east to the sea.

The land was lost, water
held its aqueous sway:
we imagined oysters
and blue whales and
crawfish and mermaids.
There were no borders
left to cross no walls
to scale no guards
to bribe no votes
to cast. The stunted
seeds we'd planted
in infertile soil
yielded nothing
but the broken
promise we'd
made to ourselves:
to leap to spawn
to never flee and
now the news
had come and
so we fled in
all directions
left the street
corner to itself
all engines idled
all tires flat
all roads closed
nothing left
but to face
the unblinking
mirror of water

Sandbar

A breach when the river rises
a beachhead when it sinks,
riverbed become batture
batture become bank
bank become levee.

She empties herself this way,
a surface that sinks beneath
itself. Her sallow skin finds
its bed of bone; flank
ceding to its bloodriver
barrier. She is a levee
of spitcurl, bellywine,
held secrets, gasps.
A girl again. I take
the beach.

No more enemies, my toes
leave no traces in the sandbar.
The river steeps, rises. I hear,
at a jaunty distance, her rippled
breathing. The warehouses are
painted in pastel colors, lie
unwashed in back-of-town
splendor. I am incapable
of drowning.

Poem

There is that shiver, the shifting
wind that knows how to make
itself gleam, the crack of violence
when earth and sea are transformed.

And so we seek the next storm,
lying in wait, tearing up some
distant shore, and envy
all those lucky bastards

quivering on the page.

Batture

April. A scrap of metal, remnant
of a long-sunken tug, coddles the
riverbank, tangles with old fishing
line, adds ballast to the batture.
It rattles in the new breeze, dogged
mortal on the river's undying flank.
Death as a sentinel against death,
life redeemed to its steadfast source.
College kids loll on the grass in
premature bikinis. A chill muffles
the supine echo of summer; cracks
appear in the riverbed, rain is denied
its reverie. Cities lay buried beneath
the oyster bed of winter, the seasons
are cantilevered. Time is moribund,
nothing occurs in stages. Each day
reaches inexorably into the next:
suddenly it rains, suddenly she
is gone, suddenly he is 50. A girl
smiles from the riverbank, evolution
is resurrected in all its imperfect glory.
The seasons know themselves again,
solitude settles into its hollow shoal,
a ripple of memory stirs
on the surface.
It is spring.

Anamnesis

You ask me to play
the penguin yet you
look to the sky.

Your tears run
on old tracks in
decaying handcars.

I sleep with wings
pasted on my
back, unflying.

We fish from
the bank, catch
nothing but nostalgia.

Later, naked,
I taste the remorse
on your skin.

Teenagers loiter
on the levee
like old cats.

Alluvion, April

The river is drunk.
Drunk on time, rain,
snowmelt, spring-
swollen memories
of winter, gorged
and gluttonous,
swallowing levees
whole, burying
the batture. Even
the catfish drown.
We stroll alongside,
shrunken, solemn,
eat nervous picnics,
drink discount wine,
stay sober and
small beside
the Great Inebriate.

Someday things,
all things, will
subside.

Storm

"unmerited salvation is also the measure of grace"
     — Robyn Creswell, review of *The Book of Travels*

We drink Moscow mules
to the myth of the City's
demise raise copper mugs
to its resurrection pray
at the altar of our own
extinction gaze at digital
photos of all our romantic
glories while the winds
whistle outside unmoor
the City from itself let
loose the ferries free
the barbarians from
their gossamer cages

but the City has good
and vigorous gills can
breathe underwater
so we surface to face
the truth with whatever
booze we can find
on our warped and
and waterlogged
shelves.

Curfew, Ida, New Orleans

They tell us we can't go
out after eight if we do
they'll shoot not to kill
but to wound but we're
wound in a cycle of
abeyance and obedience
evacuation and eviction
bedlam and blessedness
indignation and assent

so go ahead and shoot
we say you can neither
kill nor wound us this
long somnolent life
as resilient swamp
critters has rendered
us invulnerable and
you irrelevant

It's 10 P.M. We know
know where our children
are where our redemption
lies where our bodies are
buried in the sweet dark
liquid of this sweet
dark liquid night.

Spillage

She holds a cigarette
over the bath
flicks the ashes
into the water
a glow rises
on her cheek
hot ash sears
my chest
sorry she says
and sorta means it.

She reaches down,
pulls out the plug
the water drains
away leaves
me and my new
scar in the tub.

She tosses
the cigarette in
the toilet flushes
it down reaches
down pulls me
up leads me
to the bedroom.

There we conceive
our first child.

The next morning
she runs the bath.

Candles wine
epsom salts
we read archaic
poems to each other
in the lavender light

the water holds
in the tub there
is no spillage.

Seasons

Autumn arrives
without a storm
we take this
as an omen
of privilege
or nothing
in particular
our knees
entwine
like necks
of swans
which I've heard
mate for life
but I'm not
so sure and
neither
is she
is it
Mormons
or swans?
Or otters?
And what does
for life mean,
anyway?

 (I once knew
a divorced
Mormon)

We entwine
like swans,
and fuck
like otters
which I've
heard love
to fuck,
but I'm not

so sure and
neither is she
anyway

the water holds
in the tub there
is no spillage.

Afterwards, we walk
out to the swollen
river risen to
the top of
the levee
an otter clings
to a branch
whiskers attuned
to the wind and
wonders which
is safer the land
or the water

(the levee, unlike
the bath, cannot
hold the water)

The otter, mateless,
slips into the river.

Winter arrives
without warning
out on the levee
stoner dudes blast
Pearl Jam from
their pickups
film trucks
sit silently
in the zoo
parking lot
she says something

about the infusion
of fiction
with reality
the river coughs
up a dead body
I wonder if we
are a fiction
so I ask:

Are we a fiction?
Define fiction,
she says. I can't,
I say. Then,
she says, yes,
I guess we are.

Old men yank catfish
from the muddy river.

Spring arrives
the tenor of daylight
resumes. We need
cigarettes, she says.
I drive to the Circle
K. Workmen sheathed
in white dust drink
Slurpees and
eat chili dogs
in the rain.
I fill my tires
with air. I take
this as an act
of courage against
the deluge.

A block away a
pothole shreds
my tire. Too
much air, I

curse, too
much damned
air.

Honey, I say,
calling her from
a payphone.
I'll be awhile
the tire's flat.
Well she says,
no sweat. I
I won't be
here when
you get
back, But
when I
get back
she is
running
the bath.

She lights a cigarette
for me afterwards.
I take this as an act
of courage.

Lifeguard

clouds bounce
without judgment
along the surface
of the sea stories
told like sailboats
buoyed on
Biscayne Bay
the last glimmer
of November
light unleashes
constellations
of questions in
the moonless sky
we take nothing
for granted but
our own vanishing
beauty cut like
manatees beneath
the propeller blades
of speedboats in
Biscayne Bay we
sink and surface
surface and sink
restoring ourselves
to adolescent glory.

she sleeps with a boy
on the beach, they
watch the sun
rise above
the lifeguard
stand.

River: Drive

A man in
a red
hammock
wearing
a red
cap reads
a big
book baby
nestled
into his
hip his
white
dog
nestled into
the grass.

The river
is low its
bed
exposed
by drought
the carcass
of an old
boat rusts
on the shore
silhouettes
do unseen
things in
the ferns.

A tugboat
pushes a barge
there's some
thing flat
on the road
I hope it's
a scarf

DELUGE

"More bland the ichor of a ghost should run
Along your dubious veins than the rude sea…"
                    — Edna St. Vincent Millay

I. Edna, 1927

Edna, the girl from
the Gulf, gazes upriver,
not into his eyes. Her
umbrella, stubborn oyster,
cracks open on the sidewalk.
A styrofoam cup collapses
in her free hand; she steps
off the curb just outside
the picture window. She
disappears from sight; he
wonders about the lingering
power of mirages.

Edna, the girl from
the Gulf, watches, leg
pressed against itself,
the sun sink behind
the grain elevator.
A flatboat corrodes on
the riverbed, anchored
by ruin. Her thoughts
play possum with
themselves.

The rude sea pounds
in her veins; she scribbles
something about the sham
of redemption. Her fingers
are brittle white levees, they
crack at the weight of her
words, a celestial heft that

leaves blood in the margins.
The inkwell clots, a storm
surges in her womb; she
takes the ferry.

On the other side, she finds
the one with the dubious eyes
and coldsalted breath. She,
great poet, whispers something
prosaic in his direction. He,
great prosaic, heeds the poetry
in her request. Her thighs
are brittle white levees, they
crack at the weight of his
sternum, a secular heft that
leaves blood in the bedsheets.
The storm lifts, her thoughts
recede; she takes the ferry.

On the other side, she finds
the phrase with the piercing
eyes and coldsalted breath.
A pale rain splatters
on the picture
window.

*"Nothing could stand
All this rain."*

II. Rain, 1950

Nouns in New Orleans smash
into nouns gnash into nouns
slash into sounds entomb
the untombed womb the
unwombed. The knock-knock
of tugs into barges, barges into
battures, battures into bayous.

In the Great Flood the river overruns the levee and the
levee becomes the river and the river becomes the levee
and the river becomes all things and all nouns in the Great
Glory that is the river and the river becomes itself.

"Nor yet a floating spar to men that sink
And rise and sink and rise and sink again"

III. Deluge, 2005

Fearful of the breach
I keep the city in jars:
Clocks, combs, the city is
a lake-fed curio. Its breath
swells into arpeggios; relics,
plucked from the river,
sugar-sweet, drown
in the current.

The city is Vapor.
I keep it suspended,
above my head,
a twisted trumpet.
The city anoints itself.
I regard its wet carcass, cantilever
the present from the past.
The city, held above
the Earth, in jars,
dangling over
the Deluge.

"But you are mobile as the veering air,
And all your charms more changeful than the tide"

IV. Renaissance (for Fats Domino)

I hear no music in the city
of music; the drumboys
drift. The Fat Man flees,

floats to a higher octave,
a rooftop he doesn't recognize.
The Fat Man can't swim. He
has lost his syncopation, no
fever flies through his fingers,
his fingers play on mildewed
keys.

The Fat Man floats
to a higher octave.

The waters recede.
The Fat Man walks back.

"And reaching up my hand to try,
I screamed to feel it touch the sky"

Cecil B., Boca Raton

Cecil B. paddles
a red kayak in fading
sunlight, heedless
of circuses and Biblical
epics. The sea is his
template, the horizon
a huckster, the current
his only commandment.
The breeze is a bullhorn,
he speaks through sinewy
wrists turned against the
flickering sky. Jodhpur oars
tread the ingénue tide, breaker
hordes approach, await their
cue. The sea cleaves, his
breast swells with vernal
gusts. He sees the stars
concealed behind a curtain
of clouds, the Creation
that will never be His.

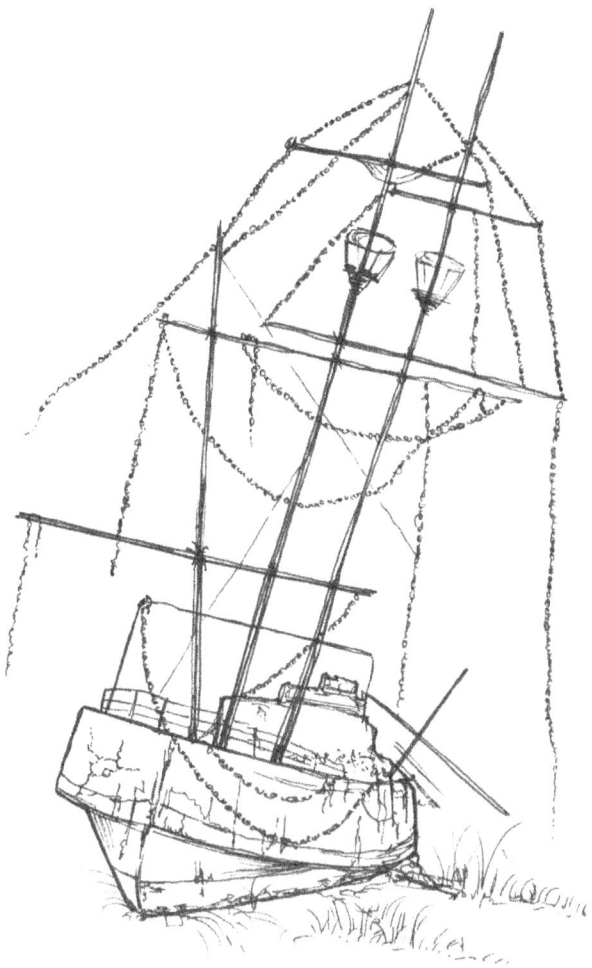

Babel IV

"To speak is to fall into tautology."
— Jorge Luis Borges

This dark, lovely mess.
Give us this day our
daily breath, our quota
of words. Give us speech,
our ration of language.
Give us words, those
incorrigible vagabonds.
Wild, irredeemable, love
crazed, unrepentant. Now
string them together, carnival
beads on a plastic necklace,
and there you have it: our
untied tongues, unloosed.
What lays buried what
is revealed.

The string breaks, and
everything's a jumble,
a listing ship, a foot
loose drunk sprawled
on the kitchen floor,
seeking the sobermad
savior of poetry.

Sirens Sweetly Singing: A Lesser Grey

The Monsignor sweeps the canyon
floor. A nun, in zumba class, sweats
out her sorrow. Six men in satin
sheets carouse in the plaza, a cat
sniffs at the balustrade. Sleep
comes to those who wait,
a peacock arouses
the dawn.

Stoner coxswains call to their crew:
"Toke!" "Toke!" Jewish girls giggle
in shul, the Rabbi shushes them in
a Hebrew they don't understand.
Methuselah drinks from the fountain
of youth, but it darkens his beard
only fifty shades of a lesser
grey.

Lambs lie down with lionesses, sheep
bleat at the cuckolded lions. Firemen
battle the Earth's final blaze, Lot's
wife pours salt on his wounds. MPs
in Parliament pass a new resolution,
reject the Second Coming, but put it
to a third referendum.

The Big Exit is nigh, typhoons
batter the coast of Ascension
Parish. Tycoons run for cover,
the rivers run in reverse. Refugees
are the new hipsters, flight the new
zeitgeist.

There is no backstop, the GOP flees
across freshly gerrymandered borders.
Bill Gates fumigates his fortune;
sixteen vestal virgins share the last

slice of shepherd's pie. Fourteen
joys and the thrill to be merry,
Tom and Aurora play the last
choro in the Backroom. Tico
tico no fubá, no one inside
notices the blasted
streets.

Face of the Poet

Each wrinkle, beveled,
earned, cantilevered
into a sparse, skeptical
smile, direct, unforced.

One crease yields
to the next, belied
by clearbright eyes,
a bounty of lines
that sing of time
lost and resurrected.

Nature's impeccable
cruelty, the face
furrowed against
gravity and grief,
each crease another
line in a poem yet
unwritten.

But the face
is enough,
the face
an epic,
the face her
masterpiece.

Death of the Poet

Last night a bloodred balloon
posing as the moon hovered
in the night sky as though it
weren't there yet it was.

Was it merely the cold
cry of the cosmos landing
in our laps a crimson
teardrop from God's
Great Face?

This morning a little
girl ambling through
the Quarter on a cold
January morning said
quite randomly to a
random couple who
she thought were her
parents but weren't:

Once I had two large
helpings of chicken
lasagna.

Moments later a man
in a speeding carriage
yelled out to no one
in particular except
perhaps to his
galloping
mule:

The word shop
comes from shogun.

This afternoon Mary Oliver
died and I wondered what

she would have made of
gluttonous orphans
chicken lasagna
runaway carriages
false etymologies.

Perhaps she would have
crafted lyrical meaning
out of cool chaos or
simply sloughed it all
off to that bloodred
balloon and said:

You're on your own.
Which is where you
ought to be: watching,
and listening.

But mostly, just
listening.

Mardi Gras, Moonwalk

"Do you know the King?"
— The Abitians

Something is left, nothing
is left, the current keeps
what the day has forgotten.

Banjo, vocoder, high
hat, dead girl, wooden
xylophone.

An orange man yells "Stella!"
from the paddlewheel. He has
never heard of Stanley Kowalski.

Sirens, drums, the relentless
roar of revelry. The river refuses
the carnival, settles into the cold
serenity of the weary sailor.

A film crew finds nothing
to film: oases make dull scenes.

A woman with a red beak
sits at my bench, asks me
for change, for a lighter,
for love.

I tell her to look at the river.

The river swells, sighs.
She says it reminds her
of a pancake. She takes
off her beak, lifts her skirt.

The force of dying
sunlight is beveled
on her breast.

The flask in my pocket
uncorks, leaks sweet
cachaça against my chest.

We make love on the cold,
hard bench. Her beak draws
blood from my cheek;
no one notices.

A freight train stalls
on the tracks; Cleopatra
and Caesar share a cigar
in its dark belly.

Across the square the cathedral
steps are cold; a sinner pens
a letter to the Pope.

Daylight finds nothing
to redeem at the altar;
it spills into the courtyard,
wakens the dead.

The sinner's words inscribe
themselves on a tombstone:

Your Holiness,
the cathedral
steps are cold.

The courtyard darkens,
the graveyard café steeps
in green and purple light.

The dead enter the café,
drink absinthe with the dead;
no one notices.

The dead order up a jazz
funeral. It slithers through
the alley:

We do not amplify only
sanctify brother spirit do
not weigh the sky only
unloose the earth do
not sanctify only
receive the rhythm do
not hue and cry only
fill the holes in our
souls.

Suppity bup bup
Sippity bip bip
Sappity bap bap
Here we come there
he goes here we
come there he
goes here we
go there he
comes here
he comes
there we
go.

I am a feather
You are a drum
I am a feather
You are a drum
God is the weather
We are his sons.

Suppity bup bup
Sippity bip bip
Sappity bap bap.

Here we come
there He goes
Here He comes
there we go.

I am unconvinced.

A quartet of large
ladies gathers on
the levee, dressed
in tutus and gold
leotards. One says:
"It's cold as death, but
I don't care." Another
says: "Let's take
a picture." The others
ignore them and waddle
upriver. The woman
with the camera says:
"They don't understand
the fucking beauty."

The sun loses its footing,
slips on a feather; the moon
takes its place. It reminds
me of a pancake. The river
swells, the woman with the red
beak gets lost in the current.

No one notices.

Ash Wednesday, Audubon Park

"Come walk with Love along the way, and O, it is a holy day."
— Minny M. Hayers

Refuse, now, is just
refuse and sin, now,
is just sin. Yesterday
the Sadist whipped the Pope,
the Pope loved on Lincoln,
and Lincoln freed the Vampire
he hunted for the Sadist. Today
a girl is just a girl; she glides
through the park in a yellow
hat and long red skirt.

Aphids cling to the oaks;
a body, caught in the thistle,
has yet to find the batture.

Children play ping-pong
on porches, Indian feathers
swirl beneath the underpass,
shopping carts stand poised
like silent Marines. Zulu
coconuts, yesterday's gold,
bleed in the trash, fleshless.

The ashes on my forehead
are just for show, the ache
in my belly is for the stupid
brown dog whose searching
eyes gaze too far into my soul.
He wears a collar of plastic pearls.

Beads dangle from the oaks,
mingle with the moss. Plagues
are now prayers, the masquerade
become morning.

A churchbell tolls on State
Street; the body swirls, refusing
to sink. Some cretin has etched
a quote by Gandhi into the bench:

Become the change you
want to see in the world.

Christ. If only I *could* change,
if only I *could* see the world.

Translation:

Impressionista (by Adelia Prado)

Uma ocasião,
meu pai pintou a casa toda
de alaranjado brilhante.
Por muito tempo moramos numa casa,
como ele mesmo dizia,
constantemente amanhecendo.

Impressionist

On a certain occasion,
my father painted our entire house
a brilliant orange.
For a long time we lived in a house,
as he liked to say,
forever dawning.

Brisa (by Manuel Bandeira)

Vamos viver no Nordeste, Anarina.
Deixarei aqui meus amigos, meus livros, minhas riquezas,
  minha vergonha.
Deixaras aqui tua filha, tua avô, teu marido, teu amante.

Aqui faz muito calor.
No Nordeste faz calor tambem.
Mas lá tem brisa:
Vamos viver de brisa, Anarina.

Breeze

Let's live in the Northeast, Anarina.
Here I will leave my friends, my books, my riches,
  my shame.
Here you will leave your daughter, your grandfather,
  your husband, your lover.

Here it is very hot.
It's hot in the Northeast too.
But there's a breeze up there.
Let's live in the breeze, Anarina.

Thrice

I imagine myself Harry Truman,
a haberdasher with an atomic bomb,
the enemy at my window, refusing
surrender, snubbing all solace, tapping
at the glass, until it shatters
on the living room floor.

Once I tell my enemy to go away
Twice I tell it to clean up its mess
Thrice I offer a truce.

But my enemy refuses:
to go away, to clean up
its mess, a truce.

And so, I nod
a haberdasher's nod:
silent, sage, resolute.

And suddenly
my enemy
vanishes.

Third time's
the charm.

Protocol, Covid-19

The   apart   ness

     the   be   in   g   a   part

the dis   tance

               be   tween   you

and   me

willwe   ev   er

   get   to

em   brace

   ?

2021

"The universe is made of stories, not atoms."
— Muriel Rukeyser

So it became October

(just as it does)

and the daylight faded

(just as it does)

but this time on

this day in this

year not so

fast not

so fast

not so

fast

The Cabin

The last poem she wrote
  sounded, when read
aloud, like a train
  heading into a tunnel:
a muffled roar receding
  into the darkness
knowing it would emerge
  again into light but
on the good, far side of things.
 She read it to me from
  a hotel room somewhere
or a hospital bed or that
  cabin at the foot
of the Flatirons where
    we last
  met and clutched
  naked and hopeless
  against the Colorado
   winter. But faith
came when she did
  and now I await
breathlessly
  the next poem.

1989, or: Her Belly Droops Over the Seat

She stands in the hallway, naked
her calves blush her
socks don't match her
nakedness is foolish and
persistent

> a voice comes over the radio:

> > this is a real revolution of the street
> > control is sliding out of our hands
> > diplomatic and grassroots events
> > seem to be on separate trains
> > running at dramatically different
> > speeds

Turn that off,
she says,
I have no patience
for diplomats who
speak the speak
through spokesmen who
speak the speak
to pressmen who
speak the speak
This, she says,
pulling up a chair,
is a *real* revolution of the street:
her belly droops over the seat.

> a voice comes over the radio:

> > and now a real revolutionary of the street
> > Amiri Baraka a.k.a. LeRoi Jones
> > He recites:
> > "…and now her belly droops over the seat

They say it's a child. But
I ain't quite so sure."

Turn that off,
she says,
I have no stomach
for poets who
speak the speak
through sonnets that
speak the speak
to scholars who
speak the speak
of *this,* she says,
contemplating her navel,
I *am* quite so sure:
her belly droops over the seat.

a voice comes over the radio:

coup in the philippines east
germany collapsing into
the west czechoslovakia
collapsing into the west
hungaryromaniabulgaria collapsing
into the west democracy
spreading like wildfire this is a
real revolution of the street chance
of showers today Mets trounce Dodgers see
the Miramax hit "Camille Claudel"

It begins to rain. The rain
is foolish and persistent she
lacquers her pursed lips with
silent deliberate swabs
of Vaseline she
associates the rain
with Rodin she
refuses to discuss
the war on any level

specific or universal she
says only: I am no Camille Claudel.
I will not be sculpted.

a voice comes over the radio:

this is a real revolution of the street
control is sliding out of our hands
diplomatic and grassroots events
seem to be on separate trains
running at dramatically different speeds

Turn that off,
she says,
We are separate trains running
at dramatically different speeds
This, she says,
packing her suitcase
is a grassroots event.

a voice comes over the radio:

diplomats poets radicals are one
this is a real revolution of the street
3 out of 4 dentists surveyed
recommend Trident for their
patients who
chew gum

Turn that off,
she says,
I have no tolerance
for dentists who-

Your father was a dentist, I say.

I know, she says,
turn it off.

I will, I say,
I promise.

Your promises are shit,
she says, lighting
a cigarette.
I can't redeem any of them.

Babel V

"…words do not live in dictionaries, they live in the mind."
— Virginia Woolf

We built the bloody
thing too damned
high, duped ourselves
along with God. We
thought we were
reaching for a better
view of us. He
thought we sought
a better view of Him.

We're too public,
too clamorous.

He's too private,
keeps His own
counsel.

Now we can barely
understand each
other, as if we
ever could. Can
someone please
write a bloody
damned poem
so we can all
at last, at least,
rhyme again?

Powder Day, Echo Mountain

The world stops turning
for a moment her eyes
shift a shade darker she
asks me if I believe in
gods or prophets I tell
her I need a bit more
evidence she holds
out her right hand
opens the palm to
reveal a new scar
then holds out her
left and asks me
to kiss her ring
the one I gave
her that she
mistook for
a talisman

and when I kiss
the ring it tastes
like a new religion
spun off the axis
of the new Earth
a moment of
shifting intent
and then, she says,
scratching her cheek
with her ring finger
baptized by my
bamboozling kiss:

Maybe we don't
really exist. Maybe
not, I say. But then
again, today is
a powder day.

We head for the slopes.
She drives.

Player, Buffa's Backroom

they tell me she's
  a prodigy a provocateur
she tells me the words

    ain't in her lexicon

      she croons a tune
      with no melody
      plays a rumba

    against her clavicle

      she sings the language
        of the firebrand
        a hotcool vernacular that bubbles

    up beneath the skin

I've heard talk of
  auras, haloes, auroras.
some claim they can

    see it from miles away.

      she snorts at such
      nonsense. I'm as
      human as the next guy,

    she says yet her breath

forms a moat of light
a perfect soundpalace
an unreachable rainbow

    I play what I play
        she says do not judge
        me except by

what you hear

she picks up her clarinet
and blasts a reply
out of beautiful, broken chords

Late: A Tableau

A clown, at Calliope, mounts
the Magazine Street bus. He
smokes a cigarette, a Camel,
unfiltered. It rains, a typhoon
rain. A pair of twins wields,
at Toledano, a tangle of ferrets,
for sale. It is morning
in New Orleans.

I am late for work.

I wonder if this, any of this,
is poetry or prose?
Would it be poetry
if the bus were heading
downtown instead of up?
Or if the cigarette were filtered,
a Dunhill instead of a Camel
Would it be prose, I wonder,
if the ferrets were cats?
Or the twins were triplets?
And what if it weren't
raining?

I am still late for work.

I wonder if this, any of this,
matters, philosophically?
I wonder if I should
wonder. And then I
remember: one must never
acclimate, if one scribbles,
to the daily phantasmagoria
of a city which is, at once,
poetry and prose. This is not
how it is everywhere else,
but it is always how it is

here. So I take out my
pen and I scribble:

*A clown, at Calliope, mounts
the Magazine Street bus...*

Eternidade
by Alberto de Lacerda

Toquei-lhe a fimbria do manto

Um quase inteiro dia

Eternity (Translation)

I touched the hem of his cloak

Almost an entire day

Eternity (after Alberto de Lacerda)

Her robe dropped to the floor.

I dropped to my knees.

Eternidade

Sua camisola caiu no chão.

Eu caí de joelhos.

Hibernation/Perennial

She likes to sleep; he
likes to let her sleep.

He knows, as she doesn't,
except in the photosynthesis
of memory, that beauty,
like sleep, is not easily
attained.

Bestowed at the source,
sustained by the seasons,
the backsweep of days,
the vigilance of foresight.

A beauty bundled and
vigorous; the abiding
rain and its sudden
absence.

Absence yields to
essence, to light, to
blooming. It is worth
the wait, he knows, so
he cuts, waters, waits.

The cuts register
on his skin, the water
fills his eyes, the wait
becomes yet another
reason to wait.

And then, the flower.

Why Is The Great American Poem
So Hard To Write?

First of all, define great. Great as in good, as
in overarching, inclusive, perfect, profound,
lovely and lean? Or at once cryptic
and coherent, the kind that provokes
nods from critics and smiles from
commoners? One that makes
children giggle and scholars
sigh? A bipartisan poem,
perhaps, now that we're lost,
chronic, incurable, terminal?
And when you say hard,
do you mean, hard
to write, imagine,
conceive, construct,
publish?

Second of all, isn't everything
hard these days, isn't everything,
these days, hard to write? I'm
sure you'll agree. And
if you don't, well, there
ya go, here we are. Okay,
so some things are easy
to write now: a polemic,
a pamphlet, a prescription;
a puffpiece, a panegyric,
a perfectly round O in
the mouth. A scream,
a screed, but a poem?
An American poem?
Good luck with that,
pal. Then how about
a lament, a hagiography,
a howl? A sob, a scar,
a suicide note? Piece

of cake, but a sonnet?
Tall order, my friend.

I could write
you, abracadabra
presto-change-o,
a postcard, a primer,
a recipe for potato
salad, a farce, a formula,
a job recommendation.
But an ode? To what?
Grief? Gamma rays?
Lady Godiva? Lady
Gaga, Good King
Wenceslas? Gas
guzzlers, single
malts, single
mothers, double
helixes? Pizza,
petrochemicals?
The NBA, NEA,
NPR, NRA? Oprah,
the opioid epidemic?
Bisons, bipods, bad
optics, biopics?

Let's try again. You
say you want a poem,
an American poem,
a revolution. Well,
ya know, we all want
to change the zeitgeist,
the prevailing narrative,
the punditry, the memeitry,
our sex, our identities,
our partners, our politics,
our citizenship, but first,
let's be honest, the playoffs
have started and we can't

just look away. Look
away, look away, look
away, look away. I wish
I were in Dixie, she was
such a lovely lady, but
a bit of a racist, dontcha
know. See what I mean?

Can we turn down the
temperature while
we turn up our noses?
Shut our ears while
we open the doors?
Open our hearts while
we lower the volume?
And then there's poetry
itself. Where is it going,
where is it taking us,
where are we taking it?
We can ask the same
questions of America,
and get no response.
Is America even
listening?

Some say its eardrums were shattered
by those hijacked planes downtown,
others say its teeth bashed in by
that con man midtown, its mouth
taped shut, its insides kicked in
by the mob that ran in his
wake, that the ink has
all run dry trying to
write about it all.

And you ask for a poem, an
American poem. Well, this,
I'm afraid, is the best I can do.

And what if I did? Wrote that damned
bloody poem, the Great American One?
What if I spat the moon onto the page
and ceased the seas from rising? What
if I scribbled refugees across the border,
melted Uzis with metaphor, beat back
the Invader with insurrectionist odes,
artilleries of alliteration, surgical
strikes of perfect verse? What if I
unmasked evil with iambics, created
a meter that sounded your car alarm,
and rescued your ride from getting jacked?
Or what if I drowned that Dodge with
oily refrains, combusted it with internal
rhymes? What if I synecdoched all sinners
and set them adrift on a lake of negation?
Or housed the sign guy on Claiborne
with homonyms, broke the Covid code
with a couplet? Could I universalize
health care with a healing phrase fumigate
fascism with free verse pulverize poverty
with pentameter neutralize neocons with nonsense?
What if I scratched out a scroll that rescued
the rivers gave succor to the seas and solidity
back to the glaciers? What if I transformed
diction into dance made licorice out of
limericks Twizzlered away all young men
from Nantucket? What if I traded
in anaphoras that fed the hungry again
again and yet again what if I eulogized
inanity lifted every other voice with
song and silenced the rest? What
if what if what if what if?

But isn't the essential thing,
when you get right down to
it (we gotta get down to it),
finding someone and something
to love, and having them love
you back? Once I loved America.

Once she loved me back. How
do you write a poem about that?

Well, this,
I'm afraid,
is the best
I can do.

Cinéma Vérité, a Glossary of Terms

Soft focus: he distrusts
memory and relies on
the memory of memory.

Wide angle: the breadth
of his longing attenuates
the gaps.

Long shot: she tumbles
into the gaps and is
nurtured there.

Jump cut: he awakens
to time and its cruel
tricks.

Tracking shot: she refuses
to exit the panorama
of his vision.

Mise en scène: what one
sees is what one sees,
and isn't.

Denouement: there is no
such thing as resolution,
only last scenes.

Moon

We the humans looked
up to see the mottled
moon in a drunken
sky only to recall
with a tincture
of regret that
we are not
alone

Morning Existential

I woke up one morning and didn't know who I was.
And then I laughed.
So I looked in the mirror and asked myself: Who are you?
And the person in the mirror laughed.
And I asked the person in the mirror why they were laughing.
And they stopped laughing.
And the person in the mirror asked me: Who are you?
And I said: I don't know.
And we both laughed.

Ecology

Falling bodies. Spiked crosses.
Sea journeys. Cracked sidewalks.
False potions. Poisoned wells.
A call to arms, all arms broken.
Dance me to the end of time.
Never mind, the music's
stopped.

119